Destination Detectives

Kenya

North
America

Europe

Asia

KENYA

Africa

South
America

Australasia

Rob Bowden

Raintree

www.raintreepublishers.co.uk
Visit our website to find out more information about **Raintree** books.

To order:
☎ Phone 44 (0) 1865 888112
🖹 Send a fax to 44 (0) 1865 314091
💻 Visit the Raintree Bookshop at **www.raintreepublishers.co.uk** to browse our catalogue and order online.

First published in Great Britain by Raintree,
Halley Court, Jordan Hill, Oxford OX2 8EJ,
Part of Harcourt Education.
Raintree is a registered trademark of
Harcourt Education Ltd.

Produced for Raintree Publishers by Discovery Books Ltd
Editorial: Clare Weaver, Sonya Newland,
Melanie Waldron, and Lucy Beevor
Design: Gary Frost and Rob Norridge
Picture Research: Amy Sparks
Production: Duncan Gilbert
Originated by Modern Age
Printed and bound in China
by South China Printing Company

10 digit ISBN 1 4062 0717 9 (hardback)
13 digit ISBN 978 1 4062 0717 0
10 9 8 7 6 5 4 3 2 1
11 10 09 08 07

10 digit ISBN 1 4062 0724 1 (paperback)
13 digit ISBN 978 1 4062 0724 8
10 9 8 7 6 5 4 3 2 1
12 11 10 09 08 07

British Library Cataloguing in Publication Data
Bowden, Rob
Kenya. - (Destination Detectives)
1. Kenya - Geography - Juvenile literature 2. Kenya -
Social life and customs - Juvenile literature 3. Kenya -
Civilization - Juvenile literature
I. Title
967.6'2043

This levelled text is a version of *Freestyle:
Destination Detectives: Kenya*, produced for Raintree
Publishers by White-Thomson Publishing Ltd.

Acknowledgements
Jonathan Bonnick pp. 38-39; Rob Bowden pp. 5, 7t,
14, 26, 29, 31t, 31b, 33, 35, 38, 40, 41; Corbis pp. 9
(Adrian Arbib), 12 (Yann Arthus-Bertrand), 16 (Carl &
Ann Purcell), 19 (Wendy Stone), 27 (Gideon Mendel); 30
(David Butow); Exile Images pp. 21 (H. Davies); Joanna
Haskova pp. 36; Marian Kaplan Photography pp. 8;
Photolibrary pp. 4 (Robert Harding Picture Library), 34
(David Cayless), 37 (Index Stock Imagery), 42 (Ariadne Van
Zandbergen), 43 (David W. Breed); Popperfoto pp. 13;
WTPix pp. 5t, 5m, 5b, 7b, 10, 11, 14-15, 17t, 17b, 18, 20-21,
22, 23, 24, 25, 28, 32, 39.

Cover photograph of Masai dance reproduced
with permission of Photolibrary/David Cayless

The paper used to print this book comes from
sustainable resources.

Contents

Any words appearing in the text in bold, **like this**, are explained in the glossary. You can also look out for them in the Word Bank box at the bottom of each page.

Where in the world?

Majestic Masai

The Masai are Kenya's best-known **ethnic group**. They share the same racial background and culture. They make a living by herding cattle. Many Masai work as **safari** guides. They take tourists to see the wildlife in Kenya's national parks.

You awake to find yourself in bed in a tent. You hear a flapping noise outside. You get up and have a look. It is dawn.

You can see a large shape between the trees. The shape moves. You hear the flapping noise again. It's an elephant flapping its ears as it walks along!

In parts of Kenya, the Masai still wear traditional dress.

WORD BANK   ethnic group people who share the same racial background and culture

A Kenyan safari

You wonder where you are. A vehicle pulls up. It has a sign on the door: *Kenya Wildlife Service – Park Ranger*. Now you know! You are in Kenya. The ranger gets out. She says, "Jambo – welcome to the Masai Mara National Park." She invites you to breakfast. Great, your tummy is rumbling!

Every year, thousands of people go on safari. They go to see wildlife in the Masai Mara National Park.

Find out later...

...which lake these flamingos live on.

...what these women are carrying.

...which animal is Kenya's top tourist attraction.

safari journey to see wildlife in its natural surroundings

A varied land

Over breakfast, the rangers tell you about Kenya. A map on the wall has notes on it. These tell you about some of the places in Kenya.

Kenya at a glance

POPULATION:
34 million

AREA:
582,646 square kilometres (224,961 square miles)

CAPITAL: Nairobi

OFFICIAL LANGUAGES:
English and Kiswahili

There are many farms around Naivasha. They grow flowers and vegetables for **export**. They are sold to countries in Europe.

The Rift Valley runs the length of Kenya. In some places, it is over 1,000 metres (3,280 feet) deep and 100 kilometres (62 miles) wide.

ETHIOPIA

Lake Turkana

UGANDA

Turkwel

RIFT VALLEY

KENYA

S O M A L I A

Kitale

Eldoret

Equator

Kisumu

Nakuru

▲ Mt Kenya

Kericho

Kisii

Naivasha

Tana

Lake Victoria

Masai Mara

Nairobi

Athi

Lamu

N
W E
S

0   200 km
0   100 miles

Tsavo

Mt Kilimanjaro ▲

Galana

Malindi

INDIAN OCEAN

TANZANIA

Mombasa

Kisumu lies on the shores of Lake Victoria. This is Africa's largest lake. Fishing is important here.

Mount Kenya is Africa's second-highest mountain. It is 5,199 metres (17,057 feet) high.

Kenya has a long coastline. It has beautiful beaches and **coral** reefs. Coral are small animals that live in the sea. A reef is a long line of coral.

WORD BANK   export selling goods to another country

Nairobi is the capital of Kenya. It is the biggest city in East Africa. 2.8 million people live there.

A rail town

Nairobi was once a swamp. The Masai used it to water their cattle. The British arrived in 1899. They were building a railway through Kenya. The railway workers lived in Nairobi. Supplies were kept there. Nairobi continued to grow. It is now one of the biggest cities in Africa.

Kenya is one of the world's biggest tea producers.

coral reef long line of coral, close to the surface of the sea

Clues from the past

One of the rangers tells you about Kenya's history. It has one of the longest human histories of any country in the world. Lake Turkana (see map, page 6) is one of the best places to learn about this. **Paleontologists** have made amazing discoveries here. They are people who study fossils to learn about life on Earth.

Human ancestors

The oldest remains of human **ancestors** have been found in East Africa. Ancestors are people we are descended from. This means we are related to them. The remains are up to six million years old!

This paleontologist holds the skulls of human ancestors discovered in Kenya.
➤

WORD BANK   paleontologist person who studies fossils to learn about the history of life on Earth

Early settlers

The Turkana people came to Lake Turkana from the Nile Valley. They came about 2,500 years ago. The way of life has changed very little. People still depend on cattle and other animals to survive. The Turkana people are cut off from the rest of Kenya. They live in simple houses called *awi*. They have no electricity or telephones.

A Turkana woman gives goats some water to drink.

▼

The Turkana

The Turkana depend on cattle and other animals for survival. They use cattle hides to make their huts. Hides are the skins of animals.

The traditional food of the Turkana also comes from cattle. It is a drink made from cows' milk and blood.

Mau Mau

The Mau Mau was a secret group of tribesmen in Kenya. They wanted to make the British leave Kenya. There was a war between the Mau Mau and the British in the 1950s. The Mau Mau lost. More than 13,000 people were killed.

Outside contact

Traders came to Kenya around 1,000 years ago. They came from the **Arabian Peninsula**. Traders are people who buy and sell goods.

In 1498, the first European reached Kenya. He was a Portuguese explorer on his way to India. His name was Vasco da Gama. By the end of the 16th century, the Portuguese controlled much of the coast.

The Portuguese built Fort Jesus in 1593. It guarded Mombasa from Arab attacks (see map, page 6).

WORD BANK Arabian Peninsula area between Africa and Asia. This includes countries like Saudi Arabia.

Colonial rule

The British took control of Kenya in 1890. They ruled for 73 years. The British started many of Kenya's industries. The tea and coffee industries are two examples. They even started tourism. People came to go on **safaris** and see the wild animals.

Independence

Kenya gained independence on 12 December 1963. British rule ended. Kenya has become one of the most important African countries.

The parliament (government) building in Nairobi (see map, page 6).

Kenya's presidents

Since independence in 1963, Kenya has had only three presidents. Jomo Kenyatta was the first. He was in power until 1978. Daniel Toroitich Arap Moi was next. Then, President Mwai Kibaki came to power in 2002.

From tip to toe

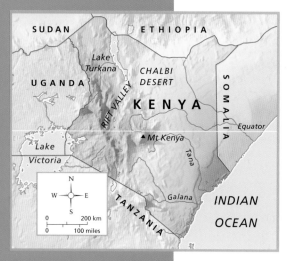

You decide to visit Mombasa on the southern coast of Kenya (see map, left). The journey from Lake Turkana will take three days.

Heat and dust

You head along the Rift Valley. The land is dry and dusty. Few people live here. It is very difficult to grow food or find water.

The temperature is over 30 °C (86 °F). It can get hotter than that before the rains come.

The Jade Sea

Lake Turkana is the largest permanent desert lake in the world. It can be very hot here. It is sometimes called the Jade Sea. This is because a plant called **algae** grows in it. It turns the water to a deep green.

A volcano next to the green waters of Lake Turkana.
➤

WORD BANK   algae small water plant

Kenya has two rainy seasons. There are long periods of rain between March and May. In October and November there are shorter rainfalls.

Cool and green

The landscape changes as you travel. It is greener. There are trees, and fields growing vegetables. You are standing on a steep cliff. These cliffs form the edges of the Rift Valley. It is cooler. You are at a higher **altitude**. Mount Kenya is 5,199 metres (17,057 feet) tall. It is the highest point in the country. There is snow on the top!

Running on high

Some of the world's best runners are from Kenya. Most come from a few tribal groups. They live high in the Rift Valley. Living at high altitude makes you fitter. This could be why Kenyan runners are so good.

This is the 3,000 metres race at the World Athletics Championship in 1999. Kenyan runner Christopher Koskei wins the gold medal.

altitude the distance above sea level

Power from below

South of Lake Naivasha there is lots of volcanic activity. The underground heat is used to make electricity.

It is made in a **geothermal** power station. Geothermal power is energy made by natural heat. Energy is used to make things work.

Western highlands

You carry on towards Nairobi through the western highlands (see map, page 6). It is an important farming area. It has good soil, warm temperatures, and year-round sun. It also has regular rainfall.

Many crops are grown for local people to eat and sell. These include maize (corn) and potatoes. Others are sold for **export**. They are sold to other countries. These include coffee and sugar. There are many **plantations** for these crops. Plantations are large farms growing just one crop.

plantation large farm growing a single crop

Around Kericho, you see green tea bushes. This is one of the world's biggest tea-producing regions.

Salt lakes

The road then heads to Nakuru (see map, page 6). There is a famous lake here. The water is very salty. **Algae** grows well in these salty conditions. The algae attracts flamingos. They come to eat the algae.

(see map, page 6)

A royal lake
Lake Victoria is Africa's largest lake. It was named after the British queen, Victoria. She was queen when the first European reached the lake in July 1858. He was a British explorer. His name was John Hanning Speke.

There can be as many as one million flamingos on Lake Nakuru at one time!

geothermal energy or source of power produced by natural heat from the ground

The highlands

You reach Nairobi. The climate is pleasant here. In the day, the temperature is around 24 °C (75 °F). But at night it can feel cold. Temperatures can drop to 5 °C (41 °F).

Savannah lands

You leave Nairobi and head to Mombasa. You enter the **savannah**. This is a grassland dotted with trees. This area is home to most of Kenya's wildlife. The road you are on passes through Tsavo National Park. It is the country's largest national park.

Wildebeest at a watering hole in the Tsavo National Park.

WORD BANK savannah tropical grassland

Coastal Kenya

The climate is hotter and humid in Mombasa. You are at sea level here. Mombasa is a busy city. To the north and south there are beautiful white-sand beaches. **Mangrove forests** are found here. Mangrove trees grow in shallow coastal waters. **Coral reefs** are also found here.

Thousands of tourists come to enjoy the beaches of Mombasa every year.

Men stack logs from the mangrove forests.

Rivers

The Tana and Galana rivers are the longest in Kenya. The Tana river has many dams built across it. They create power, which is made by the moving water. This is called **hydroelectric** power (HEP). Two-thirds of Kenya's electricity comes from HEP.

City life

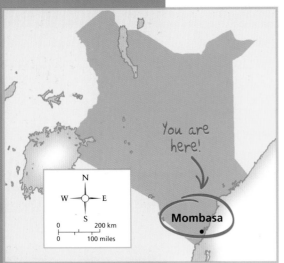

You are finally in Mombasa (see map, left). It is very busy. There are lots of people. How many are there? Where are they from? How do they live?

You see a large school building. Inside, there is a display on the wall. It is about the people of Kenya.

Mombasa is the second-largest city in Kenya. It is an important port. Ships load and unload their goods at a port.

AIDS epidemic rapid spread of AIDS, a disease caused by a virus carried in body fluids

The people of Kenya

- Kenya's population was nearly 34 million in 2005.

- By 2030, Kenya will have over 41 million people.

- 42 percent of people live in **urban** (city) areas.

- 58 percent of people live in **rural** (countryside) areas.

- The average Kenyan woman will have four children.

- Kenyans born today can expect to live for an average of only 48 years. This is because of the **AIDS epidemic**. An epidemic is when lots of people have a disease at the same time. AIDS kills many people.

You want to find out more about life in Kenya today. Nairobi is the best place to do this. It is Kenya's capital. It is also the biggest city. You decide to catch a train there.

Mixed population

Most people in Kenya are black Africans. But others are originally from the **Arabian Peninsula**, Asia, and Europe. There are:

- Around 40,000 Arabic people
- 40,000 Europeans
- 80,000 Asians.

Many black Africans are highly educated. They have specialized jobs.

rural to do with the countryside

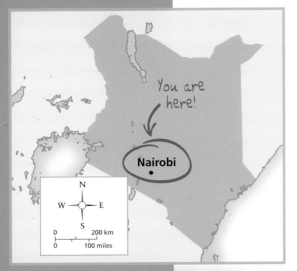

You are here!

Nairobi

N
W E
S

0   200 km
0   100 miles

Bustling Nairobi

You arrive in Nairobi on the train (see map, left). You want a good view of the city. You go to the top of the Kenyatta Conference Centre. You can see the busy city centre. There are no houses there. People live around the edges of the city.

Slum life

Nairobi has some of the worst slums in the world. At least 60 percent of the city's population live in the slums.

These tall, modern office blocks are in Nairobi's city centre.

WORD BANK   slum area of poor-quality housing

Poverty and hope

Just outside the city is Mathare Valley. This is one of Nairobi's biggest **slums**. It is an area of crowded, poor-quality housing. People here are very poor. There is no piped water or electricity. There are only a few shared toilets.

You look around. You see some children playing football. They are part of a project called Mathare Youth Sports **Association**.

Thousands of people live in slums like this one.

Easy living

Not everyone in Kenya is poor. Some people are very rich. They have expensive houses with swimming pools and gardens. They have a house staff of people to look after them.

association group of people or organizations

Improving life in the slums

You want to find out more about life in the **slums**. People are working to improve life. You talk to some of the children playing football. One of the boys takes you to see some of the work being done.

The Mathare Youth Sports **Association** (MYSA) was set up in 1987. It began as a football club for children in the slum. They still play football. They also do things to improve their slum. They clear away the rubbish. Their work is making Mathare a cleaner and safer place to live.

Boys play near one of the slums on the edge of the city.

22

environmental to do with the natural world or the conditions that surround us

People are working together in other slums, too. There are major projects to build schools and health centres.

You say goodbye to the children at Mathare. You decide to visit the **rural** areas next. Over half of Kenya's people live in the countryside.

These children have a chance of a better life thanks to the MYSA project.

23

Life in the countryside

You head north. There are fewer houses and more fields. By the roadside stalls are selling vegetables and fruit. People are also selling charcoal.

Rural life

Rural towns and villages are much smaller than the cities. There are few proper roads. You see people working in the fields. Others collect water balanced on their head.

There are small markets. People are selling things from their farms. Some are buying **provisions**. This is food and other things for the house.

Women carry goods in baskets on their heads in rural Kenya.
➤

WORD BANK provisions supplies of food and other household items

Meeting place

You stop at a market. Everyone is busy chatting. This is where everyone meets their friends. They catch up on the news. It is the centre of rural life.

A market in the Kenyan countryside. People buy and sell all sorts of goods here.

▼

End of the road

The sandal stall is one of the most popular stalls in rural markets. Old car tyres are **recycled** to make rubber sandals. People may walk many miles a day. Strong sandals are very important!

recycled used again for the same or a different use

25

Healthcare

A lady called a local **healer** sits in the market. She has piles of dried leaves, seeds, berries, and bark. These are her medicines. Local healers treat people with traditional medicines. The medicines are from plants like these. There are not many **clinics** or hospitals in **rural** areas.

There are good hospitals in the cities. They can be expensive. In the countryside, people often have to travel a long way to see a nurse or doctor. There are not enough nurses, doctors, or drugs in Kenya.

Know your plants

Local healers use plants to make traditional medicines.

Many other people in Kenya also use plants. One example is the sap from the Tumwon bush. It is used to poison arrow-tips before hunting.

Some people have to travel over 50 kilometres (30 miles) to reach a clinic like this one.

WORD BANK healer someone who treats health problems using traditional methods

Education

Primary schools are free in Kenya. But uniforms, books, and paper are not free. Some children do not go to primary school. Their parents cannot afford these things.

Secondary schools are not free. Because of this, many other children have to leave school when they are still young.

University education

Children from richer families may go on to university. Kenya's main university is the University of Nairobi. It opened in 1956. It has over 22,000 students.

Some rural schools do give a good education. This one is near Kisumu.

clinic local centre for providing basic healthcare

Transport and travel

You have noticed how many people walk places in Kenya. They walk everywhere. People walk to market, to school, to the fields, and with their animals beside them.

The long walk

Most people walk because they cannot afford other types of transport. Many people carry large items such as water cans on their heads! This is called "headloading". You need very good balance to do this!

Travelling farm

In **rural** areas, pick-up trucks are used a lot. They carry people, animals, and goods over long distances. Anything goes, as long as it can squeeze in!

Children walk along the road. They made the toys themselves.

Animal power

Donkeys are used to transport goods and people. They are good at climbing steep mountain tracks. In some places, there are no roads.

Cattle are also used to plough some fields. Tractors are now more common, though.

Gone in a flash

During the rainy season, downpours and flash floods can cause severe **landslides**. Land breaks away. Bridges are washed away. Vehicles can be stranded for days before help comes.

A train of donkeys on a mountain track in the Cherangani Hills.

landslide when a section of land breaks away

City travel

You leave the countryside. You head back to the cities. You want to find out about other types of transport. You catch a brightly painted bus. It is going to the city of Eldoret (see map, page 6). The roads are busy with cars and buses. You cross a railway line. There is an airport sign.

Transport system

Transport hubs (centres) are where different types of transport come together. You can travel to them by road, rail, and air. The main hubs in Kenya are the cities of Nairobi, Mombasa, Kisumu, Eldoret, and Nakuru.

Boda bodas

Boda bodas are bicycle taxis. The passenger sits on the back. They are cheap and very popular. They used to carry people from border to border between Kenya and Uganda. That is how they got their name.

Nairobi is Kenya's most important transport hub. The streets are crowded with cars and trucks.

Local travel

From each transport hub, local transport services go to villages and smaller towns. Buses and shared taxis travel to remote areas. The *matatu* is the most common type of public transport in cities. A *matatu* is a small minibus.

These are *tuk-tuks*. They are three-wheeled vehicles. They are used as taxis.

Today, Kenya's railways mainly carry goods.

End of the line?

The railway opened up Kenya to the outside world. It was once an important trade route. Today, there are very few services. Much of the railway is in poor condition.

Food and culture

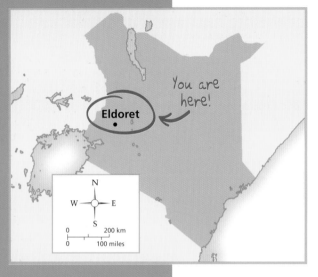

You are here!

Eldoret

N
W E
S

0   200 km
0   100 miles

The journey to Eldoret has made you hungry. You set off for some food. There is a lot of choice – pizzas, burgers, and Indian food. There are many local dishes, too.

Meat feast

Kenyans enjoy eating meat. In Nairobi there is a restaurant called Carnivore. Here you can try zebra, giraffe, ostrich, and other game (meat). It is the ultimate meat feast!

Beans for sale at a market. All sorts of food can be bought fresh at markets in Kenya.

▼

skewer metal or wooden rod for holding meat during cooking

Karibuni Diner Menu

MEAT AND FISH DISHES

NYAMA CHOMA – roasted meat
  (can be goat, mutton, or beef)
MUSHKAKI – small pieces of meat
  cooked on **skewers** (like kebabs)
TILAPIA – a meaty white fish
  from Lake Victoria, grilled whole

VEGETABLE DISHES

IRIO – potato, cabbage, and beans
  mashed together
UGALI – ground maize (corn) boiled
  with water (sometimes milk) into a
  solid paste
MATOKE – mashed **plantain**

SNACKS

MKATE MAYAI – thin pancake
  bread wrapped around a fried egg
  and minced meat
MANDAZI – deep fried sweet dough
  (similar to a doughnut)

FRUITS

MAEMBE – mango
MACHUNGWA – oranges
NDIZI – banana
PAPAI – papaya

DRINKS

MAZIWALALA – fermented milk
CHAI – tea
KAHAWA – coffee

Maize is ground in a maize mill. It is boiled up with water to make *ugali*. This is a popular dish.

◄

plantain green fruit like a banana

Kenyan dancing

You hear a mix of Western and Kenyan pop music being played. This has replaced a lot of traditional music. Traditional dance and fashion have also been replaced. Some customs still remain, though.

The Masai and Samburu people are famous for their leaping dance. They jump into the air while they chant and sing. Men perform the dance. It is a popular tourist attraction. Some dancing is performed with drumming.

Masai men perform their jumping dance.

➤

Fashion

Many Kenyan people wear Western clothes. They wear jeans and T-shirts. Some traditional clothing is, however, still worn.

Women wear the *kanga*. It is a cotton wrap. It is normally brightly coloured. Men wear the *kikoi*. It is a wrap worn around the lower body. Older men and men who live in **rural** areas tend to wear the *kikoi*.

Women of the Pokot people wear elaborate bead necklaces.

Wildlife and tourism

Tourism is very important to Kenya. You visit the tourist office in Eldoret to find out more.

Safari tour

On a 10-day safari tour you will see wildlife in national parks. You will also visit a Masai village. You will stay in luxury rooms. You may also go shopping. Or you might relax on a Mombasa beach for a few days.

On tour

Most tourists come to Kenya to see the wildlife. The lady in the tourist office tells you there are many other things to do. You can explore the towns and beaches. You can climb mountains.

In some parts of Kenya, there are large workshops. People make souvenirs for tourists to buy.

Call of the wild

Kenya has the world's largest number of mammals in one place. You hear **safaris** are a wonderful experience. You decide to see for yourself. You join a safari tour to the Amboseli National Park. You hope to see elephants and lions.

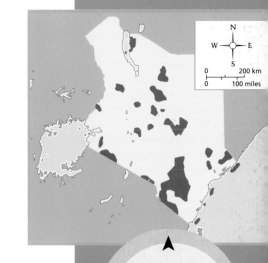

The main national parks and reserves in Kenya.

Safari tours take you out in jeeps to see Kenya's wildlife.

Trekking

There are lots of mountains in Kenya where you can go trekking (hiking). A trek to the top of Mount Kenya takes about four days. Some treks in the Cherangani Hills can be done in about a day.

People and wildlife

Amboseli National Park is one of the top tourist attractions in Kenya. It is famous for its large elephant herds.

The Masai have grazed their cattle here for hundreds of years. In 1970 parts of the area were set aside for wildlife. The Masai were angry. They had lost their land. They killed many wild animals. The **government** gave them some of their land back. The Masai live peacefully again.

Hunting the "Big Five"

In the past, Kenya was popular with **safari** hunters. They hunted and killed animals. The elephant, rhino, lion, leopard, and buffalo were the most prized animals. They were known as the "Big Five".

Ecotourists unload a truck near Eldoret.

Valuing wildlife

People are clearing land for housing and farmland in many parts of Kenya. Wildlife is forced into areas where people live. This causes problems. Farmland is destroyed. Livestock is killed.

So, some people have decided to live alongside the wildlife. They have opened their land to tourists. They can make money from tourists who come to see the animals. This is called **ecotourism**. It helps people and animals.

Lions were once hunted as one of Kenya's "Big Five".

A herd of elephants tramples vegetation in the Amboseli National Park.

ecotourism tourism that helps local people and does not harm the environment

Conserving wildlife

You are back at one of the **safari** lodges in Amboseli. You decide to go to a talk about protecting wildlife.

Much of Kenya's wildlife is under threat from human beings. This happens even in the national parks. Tourists can upset animals' way of life.

Elephants in Amboseli National Park. Mount Kilimanjaro (in Tanzania) is in the background.

▼

Special action has been taken to protect some animals. The rhino is one of the most endangered animals in the world. This means it is in danger of disappearing forever. Lake Nakuru National Park has an electric fence all the way around it. It is to stop people called **poachers** from hunting and stealing the rhinos.

In Tsavo National Park poachers hunt elephants for their ivory. Armed guards try to protect the elephants.

Shop carefully

Wildlife is sometimes killed to make souvenirs. Crocodile skin can be used to make bags. Ivory from elephants is used to make carvings. These goods are **illegal**. You should not buy them.

This is a conservation area for endangered (under threat) rhinos. It has been set up at Lake Nakuru.

poacher someone who kills and steals protected animals from the wild

41

Stay or go?

You catch a flight to Mombasa. You end your journey around Kenya relaxing on the beach. If you want to go home, the airport is nearby. What could you do if you choose to stay?

Still to see and do

You could:

• Take a camel **safari**.

• Visit the Samburu people.

• Watch a game of football, cricket, or polo in one of the large sports stadiums.

You could visit the Samburu people. Watch their traditional dancing.

- Sail along the Kenyan coast in a boat called a **dhow**.

- Trek up Mount Kenya. It is the second-highest point in Africa.

- Camp in Kakamega rainforest. It is the last remaining rainforest in Kenya.

- Go fishing on Lake Victoria. A fish called the giant Nile Perch lives here. Big ones can weigh more than a human adult!

Locals go fishing on Lake Victoria.

Find out more

World Wide Web

If you want to find out more about Kenya, you can search the Internet. Try using keywords, such as these:

- Kenya
- Nairobi
- Masai

You can also find your own keywords by using words from this book. Try using a search directory such as www.yahooligans .com

Are there ways for a Destination Detective to find out more about Kenya? Yes! Check out the books listed below.

Further reading

Countries of the World: Kenya, Rob Bowden (Evans Brothers, 2002)

Country Studies: Kenya, Heather Blades (Heinemann Library, 2001)

Country File: Kenya, Ian Graham (Franklin Watts, 2003)

Nations of the World: Kenya, Bridget Giles (Raintree, 2003)

The Changing Face of: Kenya, Rob Bowden (Hodder Wayland, 2002)

World Tour: Kenya, Patrick Daley (Raintree, 2003)

Timeline

Around AD 900
Arabian and Persian travellers travel to East Africa.

1498
Portuguese explorer Vasco da Gama reaches East Africa.

1593
Mombasa becomes the centre of Portuguese power in East Africa.

1847
European missionaries (people sent to do religious work) start travelling in Kenya.

1886
The British gain control of Kenya.

1905
British settlers experiment with growing coffee in Kenya.

1907
Nairobi becomes the centre of British power in Kenya.

1923
First tea **plantation** is set up in Kenya.

1944
Kenyan African Union is formed to campaign for African independence.

1952
Mau Maus begin to attack white settlers.

1960
Skull of ancient man discovered near Turkana in northern Kenya. He is believed to be 1.8 million years old.

1963
Kenya gains independence from British rule.

1977
A new law bans hunting big game animals, such as lions and elephants.

1978
Kenya's first president Jomo Kenyatta dies. Daniel Arap Moi becomes president.

1979
A campaign is launched for the protection of rhinos in Kenya.

1997
Severe floods in Kenya leave thousands of people homeless.

1998
A bomb attack by terrorists on the US Embassy in Nairobi kills 224 people. Most of them are Kenyans.

2001
Severe drought in northern Kenya. Millions of people starve.

2002
Mwai Kibaki becomes president.

2006
Another severe drought in northern Kenya. Four million people need food aid.

plantation large farm growing a single crop

Kenya – facts & figures

The black stripe on the Kenyan flag represents the African people. The red stripe stands for the struggle for independence. The green represents agriculture. The thin white stripes symbolize peace and unity. The warrior's shield covering crossed spears represent Kenya's fight for freedom.

Technology boom

- Internet users: 400,000.
- Telephone lines: 328,400.
- Mobile phones: 1,590,800.
- Internet country code: .ke

Trade and industry

- Main **exports**: tea, coffee, fruit and vegetables, fish.
- Main **imports**: machinery and transport equipment.

People and places

- Population: 34 million.
- Life expectancy: men – 49 years; women – 47 years.
- Highest point: Mount Kenya (5,199 metres/ 17,057 feet).

Glossary

AIDS epidemic rapid spread of AIDS, a disease caused by a virus carried in body fluids

algae small water plant

altitude the distance above sea level

ancestor person from whom you are descended

Arabian Peninsula area between Africa and Asia. This includes countries like Saudi Arabia.

association group of people or organizations

clinic local centre for providing basic healthcare

coral reef long line of coral, close to the surface of the sea

dhow type of sail boat

ecotourism tourism that helps local people and does not harm the environment

environment the natural world or the conditions that surround us

ethnic group people who share the same racial background and culture

export selling goods to another country

geothermal energy or source of power produced by natural heat from the ground

government group of people that makes laws and manages the country

healer someone who treats health problems using traditional methods

hydroelectric power created by moving water

illegal against the law

imports goods brought in from another country

landslide when a section of land breaks away

mangrove forest type of tropical forest that grows in shallow coastal waters

paleontologist person who studies fossils to learn about the history of life on Earth

plantain green fruit like a banana

plantation large farm growing a single crop

poacher someone who kills and steals protected animals from the wild

provisions supplies of food and other household items

recycled used again for the same or a different use

rural to do with the countryside

safari journey to see wildlife in its natural surroundings

savannah tropical grassland

skewer metal or wooden rod for holding meat during cooking

slum area of poor-quality housing

urban to do with cities

Index